The Institute of Chartered Accountants in England and Wales

ASSURANCE

For exams in 2016

Study Manual

www.icaew.com

Assurance
The Institute of Chartered Accountants in England and Wales

ISBN: 978-1-78363-199-5

Previous ISBN: 978-0-85760-979-3

First edition 2007

Ninth edition 2015

The content of this publication is intended to prepare students for the ICAEW examinations, and should not be used as professional advice.

British Library Cataloguing-in-Publication Data
A catalogue record for this book has been applied for from the British Library

Originally printed in the United Kingdom by Polestar Wheatons on paper obtained from traceable, sustainable sources.

Polestar Wheatons
Hennock Road
Marsh Barton
Exeter
EX2 8RP

Welcome to ICAEW

I am delighted that you have chosen ICAEW to progress your journey towards joining the chartered accountancy profession. It is one of the best decisions I also made.

The role of the accountancy profession in the world's economies has never been more important. People making financial decisions need knowledge and guidance based on the highest technical and ethical standards. ICAEW Chartered Accountants provide this better than anyone. They challenge people and organisations to think and act differently, to provide clarity and rigour, and so help create and sustain prosperity all over the world.

As a world leader of the accountancy and finance profession, we are proud to promote, develop and support over 144,000 chartered accountants worldwide. Our members have the knowledge, skills and commitment to maintain the highest professional standards and integrity. They are part of something special, and now, so are you. It's with our support and dedication that our members and hopefully yourself, will realise career ambitions, maintain a professional edge and contribute to the profession.

You are now on your journey towards joining the accountancy profession, and a highly rewarding career with endless opportunities. So, if you are studying for our Certificate in Finance, Accounting and Business (ICAEW CFAB) or our world-leading chartered accountancy qualification, the ACA, you too have made the first of many great decisions in your career.

You are in good company, with a network of over 26,000 students around the world made up of like-minded people, you are all supported by ICAEW. We are here to support you as you progress through your studies and career we will be with you every step of the way, visit page ix to review the key resources available as you study.

I wish you the best of luck with your studies and look forward to welcoming you to the profession in the future.

Michael Izza
Chief Executive
ICAEW

Contents

1 Introduction

ACA qualification

The ICAEW chartered accountancy qualification, the ACA, is a world-leading professional qualification in accountancy, finance and business.

The ACA has integrated components that give you an in-depth understanding across accountancy, finance and business. Combined, they help build the technical knowledge, professional skills and practical experience needed to become an ICAEW Chartered Accountant.

Each component is designed to complement each other, which means that you can put theory into practice and you can understand and apply what you learn to your day-to-day work. Progression through all the elements of the ACA simultaneously will enable you to be more successful in the workplace and exams.

The components are:

* Professional development
* Ethics and professional scepticism
* 3-5 years practical work experience
* 15 accountancy, finance and business modules

To find out more on the components of the ACA and what is involved in training, visit your dashboard at icaew.com/dashboard.

ICAEW Certificate in Finance, Accounting and Business

The ICAEW Certificate in Finance, Accounting and Business (ICAEW CFAB) teaches essential skills and knowledge in the three key areas of finance, accounting and business.

ICAEW CFAB consists of the same six modules as the first level of our world-leading qualification, the ACA. This means, it can serve as a stand-alone qualification or as a stepping stone on your journey towards chartered accountancy.

You can find out more about the ICAEW CFAB exams and syllabus at icaew.com/cfabstudents.

To learn more about the ACA qualification and chartered accountancy, visit icaew.com/careers.

2 Assurance

The full syllabus and technical knowledge grids can be found within the module study guide. Visit icaew.com/dashboard for this and more resources.

2.1 Module aim

To ensure that students understand the assurance process and fundamental principles of ethics, and are able to contribute to the assessment of internal controls and gathering of evidence on an assurance engagement.

2.2 Method of Assessment

The Assurance module is assessed by a 1.5 hour computer-based exam. The exam consists of 50 questions worth two marks each, covering the areas of the syllabus in accordance with the weightings set out in the specification grid. The questions are presented in the form of multiple choice, multi-part multiple choice, or multiple response.

2.3 Specification grid

This grid shows the relative weightings of subjects within this module and should guide the relative study time spent on each. Over time the marks available in the assessment will equate to the weightings below, while slight variations may occur in individual assessments to enable suitably rigorous questions to be set.

		Weighting (%)
1	The concept, process and need for assurance	20
2	Internal controls	25
3	Gathering evidence on an assurance engagement	35
4	Professional ethics	20
		100

3 Key Resources

Student support team

Our student support team are here to help you, providing full support throughout your studies.

T +44 (0)1908 248 250
F +44 (0)1908 248 069
E studentsupport@icaew.com

Student website

The student area of our website provides the latest information, guidance and exclusive resources to help you as you progress through the ACA. Find everything you need at icaew.com/dashboard.

If you are studying for the ICAEW CFAB qualification, you can access exam resources and support at icaew.com/cfab.

Online student community

The online student community provides support and practical advice – wherever you are, whenever you need it. With regular blogs covering a range of work, life and study topics as well as a forum where you can post your questions and share your own tips. ACA and ICAEW CFAB students can join the conversation at icaew.com/studentcommunity.

Tuition

The ICAEW Partner in Learning scheme recognises tuition providers who comply with our core principles of quality course delivery. If you are receiving structured tuition with an ICAEW Partner in Learning, make sure you know how and when you can contact your tutors for extra help. If you are not receiving structured tuition and are interested in classroom, online or distance learning tuition, take a look at our recognised Partner in Learning tuition providers in your area, on our website icaew.com/dashboard.

Faculties and Special Interest Groups

Faculties and special interest groups support and develop members and students in areas of work and industry sectors that are of particular interest.

Our seven faculties provide knowledge, events and essential technical resources. As an ACA or ICAEW CFAB student, you can register to receive a complimentary e-newsletter from one faculty of your choice each year throughout your studies.

Find out more about faculties and special interest groups at icaew.com/facultiesandsigs.

Library & Information Service (LIS)

The Library & Information Service is ICAEW's world-leading accountancy and business library. The library provides access to thousands of resources online and a document delivery service, you'll be sure to find a useful eBook, relevant article or industry guide to help you. Find out more at icaew.com/library.

CHAPTER 1

Concept of and need for assurance

Introduction

Examination context

Topic List

    1   What is assurance?

    2   Why is assurance important?

    3   Why can assurance never be absolute?

    4   The statutory audit

Summary and Self-test

Answers to Interactive questions

Answers to Self-test

Introduction

Learning objectives

- Understand the concept of assurance ☐

- Recognise the criteria which constitute an assurance engagement ☐

- Recognise subject matter suitable to be the subject of an assurance engagement ☐

- Understand the different levels of assurance that can be provided in an assurance engagement, including reasonable assurance ☐

- Understand the need for professional accountants to carry out assurance work in the public interest ☐

- Understand the meaning of 'a true and fair view' ☐

- Understand why users desire assurance reports and recognise examples of the benefits gained from them such as to assure the quality of an entity's published corporate responsibility or sustainability report ☐

- Compare the functions and responsibilities of the different parties involved in an assurance engagement ☐

- Understand the issues which can lead to gaps between the outcomes delivered by the assurance engagement and the expectations of users of the assurance reports ☐

- Identify how these 'expectations gaps' can be overcome ☐

Specific syllabus references for this chapter are: 1a, b, c, d, e, h.

Syllabus links

You have studied the basic books, records and financial statements of a company in the Accounting paper. It is in relation to these records that the auditor will seek evidence to be able to give assurance.

As already mentioned, audit is a key form of assurance and you will be able to apply the basic principles learnt in this paper to that form of assurance service both here and in the Audit and Assurance Paper.

Examination context

It is crucial to the whole syllabus that you understand the concept of assurance, why it is required and the reason for assurance engagements being carried out by appropriately qualified professionals. You can therefore expect to see questions in the exam testing your understanding of the definition of assurance and the different levels of assurance.

In the sample paper, the first five questions relate to the subject matter you will cover in this chapter.

In the assessment, candidates may be required to:

- Describe the concept of assurance

- State the benefits of an assurance report

- Compare the functions and responsibilities of the different parties involved in an assurance engagement

- Describe the levels of assurance obtained from different types of assurance engagement

- Describe the concept of the 'expectations gap'

1 What is assurance?

Section overview

- An assurance engagement is one in which a practitioner expresses a conclusion, designed to enhance the degree of confidence of the intended users, other than the responsible party, about the outcome of the evaluation or measurement of a subject matter against criteria.

- Key elements are: three party involvement, subject matter, suitable criteria, sufficient appropriate evidence, written report.

- Assurance engagements can give either a reasonable level of assurance or a limited level of assurance.

- There are various examples of assurance services, the key example in the UK is the audit.

1.1 Definition (parties, subject matter, criteria)

Definition

An **assurance engagement** is one in which a practitioner expresses a conclusion designed to enhance the degree of confidence of the intended users other than the responsible party about the outcome of the evaluation or measurement of a subject matter against criteria.

The key elements of an assurance engagement are as follows:

- Three people or groups of people involved

    - The practitioner (accountant)
    - The intended users
    - The responsible party (the person(s) who prepared the subject matter)

- A subject matter

    As we shall see below, the subject matter of an assurance engagement may vary considerably. However, it is likely to fall into one of three categories:

    - Data (for example, financial statements or business projections)
    - Systems or processes (for example, internal control systems or computer systems)
    - Behaviour (for example, social and environmental performance or corporate governance)

- Suitable criteria

    The person providing the assurance must have something by which to judge whether the information is reliable and can be trusted. So for example, in an assurance engagement relating to financial statements, the criteria might be accounting standards. The practitioner will be able to test whether the financial statements have been put together in accordance with accounting standards, and if they have, then the practitioner can conclude that there is a degree of assurance that they are reliable.

    In the context of company behaviour, suitable criteria to judge whether something is reliable and can be trusted might be the UK Corporate Governance Code, or, if the company has one, its published Code of Practice.

- Sufficient appropriate evidence to support the assurance opinion

    The practitioner must substantiate the opinion that he draws in order that the user can have confidence that it is reliable. The practitioner must obtain evidence as to whether the criteria have been met. We will look at the collection of evidence in detail later in this Study Manual.

- A written report in appropriate form

Lastly, it is required that assurance reports are provided to the intended users in a written form and contain certain specified information. This adds to the assurance that the user is being given, as it ensures that key information is being given and that the assurance given is clear and unequivocal.

Worked example: Assurance engagement

In order to demonstrate these elements of an assurance engagement, the Worked example is that of a house purchase. Imagine you are buying a house. There are certain issues you would want assurance about, particularly whether the house is structurally sound. In this situation, you would be unlikely just to trust the word of the person who was selling the house but would seek the additional assurance of a qualified professional, such as a surveyor.

You should already be able to see the first key element of an assurance engagement, which is the involvement of three people:

- You (the intended user)
- The house owner (the responsible party)
- The surveyor (the practitioner)

The subject matter of this assurance engagement is the house in question. The surveyor will visit the house to test whether it is sound and will draw a conclusion.

The surveyor will judge whether the house is sound in the context of building regulations, planning rules and best practice in the building industry. These are the criteria by which he will judge whether he can give you assurance that the house is structurally sound.

In order to make a conclusion, the surveyor will obtain evidence from the house (for example, by looking for damp patches and making inspections of key elements of the house).

Lastly, when he has drawn a conclusion, the surveyor will issue a report to you, outlining his opinion as to whether the house is sound or not. This report will contain any limitations to his work, for example, if he was unable to access any of the property or he was unable to lift fitted carpets to inspect the floor underneath them.

Ultimately, when you have read the surveyor's report, you will have more assurance about the state of the property, and correspondingly, more confidence to pay the deposit, take out a mortgage and buy that house.

Interactive question 1: Assurance engagement   [Difficulty level: Easy]

You are an accountant who has been approached by Jamal, who wants to invest in Company X. He has asked you for assurance whether the most recent financial statements of Company X are a reliable basis for him to make his investment decision.

Identify the key elements of an assurance engagement in this scenario, if you accepted the engagement.

See **Answer** at the end of this chapter.

1.2 Levels of assurance

The definition of an assurance engagement given above is taken from the International Framework for Assurance Engagements, which is issued by the International Federation of Accountants (IFAC), a global organisation for the accountancy profession, which works with its member organisations to protect the public interest by encouraging high quality practices around the world. ICAEW is a member of IFAC.

The Framework identifies two types of assurance engagement:

- Reasonable assurance engagement
- Limited assurance engagement

Definitions

Reasonable assurance: A high level of assurance, that is less than absolute assurance, that engagement risk has been reduced to an acceptably low level, which then allows a conclusion to be expressed positively.

Limited assurance: A meaningful level of assurance, that is more than inconsequential but is less than reasonable assurance, that engagement risk has been reduced to an acceptable level, which then allows a conclusion to be expressed negatively.

The reason that there are two types of assurance engagement is that the level of assurance that can be given depends on the evidence that can be obtained by the practitioner. Using the surveyor example above, a surveyor can only give assurance that a property is structurally sound if he is allowed to enter the property to inspect it. If he is only given access to part of the building, he can only give limited assurance.

The key differences between the two types of assurance engagement are therefore:

- The evidence obtained
- The type of opinion given

We shall look in detail at obtaining evidence later in this Study Manual. The key point about evidence is that in all assurance engagements, sufficient, appropriate evidence must be obtained. We will look at what constitutes sufficient, appropriate evidence as we go through the course. What determines whether evidence is sufficient and appropriate is the level of assurance that the practitioner is trying to give, so it is tied in with the type of opinion being given, which we shall look at here. In summary, a lower level of evidence will be obtained for a limited assurance engagement.

The opinion given in an assurance engagement therefore depends on what type of engagement it is. As noted above, there are two levels of assurance expressed positively and negatively.

Say, for example, that a practitioner is seeking evidence to conclude whether the report issued by the Chairman of a company in the financial statements is reasonable or not. He could seek evidence, conclude that the statement is reasonable and state in a report something like this:

'In my opinion, the statement by the Chairman regarding X is reasonable'.

This is a positive statement of his conclusion that the statement is reasonable. Alternatively, he could state in a report something like this:

'In the course of my seeking evidence about the statement by the Chairman, nothing has come to my attention indicating that the statement is not reasonable.'

This conclusion is less certain, as it implies that matters could exist which cause the statement to be unreasonable, but that the practitioner has not uncovered any such matters. This is therefore called limited assurance. It is the conclusion that a practitioner gives when he carries out a limited assurance engagement and seeks a lower level of evidence.

SUMMARY OF TYPES OF ENGAGEMENT		
Type of engagement	Evidence sought	Conclusion given
Reasonable assurance	Sufficient and appropriate	Positive wording
Limited assurance	Sufficient and appropriate (lower level)	Negative wording

1.3 Examples of assurance engagements

The key example of an assurance engagement in the UK is a statutory audit. We shall look at the nature of this engagement later on in this chapter.

Other examples of assurance engagements include other audits, which may be specialised due to the nature of the business, for example:

- Local authority audits (audits of local authorities, with specific reporting requirements which differ from the statutory audit)

- Insurance company audits, bank audits, pension scheme audits (audits of often complex companies in a highly-regulated industry)

- Charity audits (charities may be audited under the Companies Act or the Charities Act)

- Solicitors' audits (audits of firms of solicitors in line with the Solicitors' Accounts Rules)

- Branch audit (where an overseas company trades in the UK through a branch and requires an audit of that branch although an audit is not required by UK law)

There are also many issues users want assurance on, where the terms of the engagement will be agreed between the practitioner and the person commissioning the report, for example:

- Value for money studies (for example, in the public sector where auditors may be asked to conclude on whether a service provides value for money)

- Environmental audits (assurance engagements on information given about an organisation's impact on the natural environment)

- Internal audit

- Circulation reports (for example, for magazines)

- Cost/benefit reports

- Due diligence (where a report is requested on an acquisition target)

- Reviews of specialist business activities

- Reports on website security, such as WebTrust

- Fraud investigations

- Inventories and receivables reports

- Internal control reports

- Reports on business plans or projections

2 Why is assurance important?

Section overview

- Who the users are will depend on the nature of the subject matter.
- Users benefit from receiving an independent, professional opinion on the subject matter.
- Users may also benefit from additional confidence in the subject matter given to others.
- The existence of an assurance service may prevent errors or frauds occurring in the first place.

2.1 Users

In the key assurance service of audit, which we looked at above, the users were the shareholders of a company, to whom the financial statements are addressed. In other cases, the users might be the board of directors of a company or a subsection of them.

2.2 Benefits of assurance

The key benefit of assurance is the **independent, professional verification** being given to the users. This can be seen in the example of the house purchase given above. The importance of independence and objectivity in assurance provision will be looked at in Chapters 14 and 15.

In addition, assurance may have subsidiary benefits.

Although an assurance report may only be addressed to one set of people, it may give additional confidence to other parties in a way that benefits the business. For example, audit reports are addressed to shareholders, but the existence of an unqualified audit report might give the bank more confidence to lend money to that business, in other words, it enhances the credibility of the information.

The existence of an independent check might help prevent errors or frauds being made and reduce the risk of management bias. In other words, the fact that an assurance service will be carried out might make people involved in preparing the subject matter more careful in its preparation and reduce the chance of errors arising. Therefore it can be seen that an assurance service may act as a deterrent.

In addition, where problems exist within information, the existence of an assurance report draws attention to the deficiencies in that information, so that users know what those deficiencies are.

Assurance is also important in more general terms. It helps to ensure that high quality, reliable information exists, leading to effective markets that investors have faith in and trust. It adds to the reputation of organisations and even countries, so that investors are happy to invest in country X because there is a strong culture of assurance provision there.

Businesses are keen to be seen as acting responsibly and are increasingly publishing information such as emissions targets or a pledge not to employ children. There is a growing public perception that this is an important area and stakeholders are unlikely to associate with businesses that could damage their reputation. Corporate responsibility or sustainability reports provide assurance for stakeholders that this published information is reliable and accurate.

3 Why can assurance never be absolute?

Section overview

- Assurance can never be absolute.
- Assurance provision has limitations which may not be understood by users.
- The expectations gap also adds to the lack of guarantee given by assurance.

Assurance can never be absolute. Assurance providers will never give a certification of absolute correctness due to the limitations set out below.

3.1 Limitations of assurance

A key issue for accountants is that there are limitations to assurance services, and therefore there is always a risk involved that the wrong conclusion will be drawn. We shall look in more detail at this issue of assurance engagement risk in Chapter 3.

The limitations of assurance services include:

- The fact that testing is used – the auditors do not oversee the process of building the financial statements from start to finish.

- The fact that the accounting systems on which assurance providers may place a degree of reliance also have inherent limitations (we shall look at control systems and their limitations in Chapter 5).

- The fact that most audit evidence is persuasive rather than conclusive.

- The fact that assurance providers would not test every item in the subject matter (this would be prohibitively expensive for the responsible party, so a sampling approach is used – see Chapter 11).

- The fact that the client's staff members may collude in fraud that can then be deliberately hidden from the auditor or misrepresent matters to them for the same purpose.

- The fact that assurance provision can be subjective and professional judgements have to be made (for example, about what aspects of the subject matter are the most important, how much evidence to obtain, etc).

- The fact that assurance providers rely on the responsible party and its staff to provide correct information, which in some cases may be impossible to verify by other means.

- The fact that some items in the subject matter may be estimates and are therefore uncertain. It is impossible to conclude absolutely that judgemental estimates are correct.

- The fact that the nature of the assurance report might itself be limiting, as every judgement and conclusion the assurance provider has drawn cannot be included in it.

3.2 The expectations gap

The problems users may experience in connection with assurance provision also arise from the limitations and restrictions inherent in assurance provision. This is often because users are not aware of the nature of the limitations on assurance provision, or do not understand them and believe that the assurance provider is offering a service (such as a guarantee of correctness) which in fact he is not.

The distinction between reasonable and limited assurance may also be misunderstood by users.

We shall look at the concept of the expectations gap in more detail in Chapter 4, in the context of reporting, but in essence it is this lack of understanding which constitutes the expectations gap – meaning that there is a gap between what the assurance provider understands he is doing and what the user of the information believes he is doing.

Assurance providers need to close this gap as far as possible in order to maintain the value of the assurance provided for the user. This is done in a variety of ways, for example, by issuing an engagement letter spelling out the work that will be carried out and the limitations of that work (which we shall look at in the next chapter) and by regularly reviewing the format and content of reports issued as a result of assurance work.

Interactive question 2: Benefits of assurance   [Difficulty level: Exam standard]

Which **three** of the following are benefits of assurance work?

	An independent, professional opinion
	Additional confidence given to other related parties
	Testing as a result of sampling is cheaper for the responsible party
	Judgements on estimates can be conclusive
	Assurance may act as a deterrent to error or fraud

See **Answer** at the end of this chapter.

4 The statutory audit

Section overview

- The statutory audit is the key example of an assurance engagement in the UK.
- Auditors are subject to a variety of legal and professional requirements.
- Audits are composed of five principal stages: obtaining the engagement, planning, procedures, review, and reporting.
- Professional scepticism is an important aspect of the auditor's skillset.

4.1 Statutory audit

An audit is historically the most important type of assurance service in the UK. This is because it is a legal (statutory) requirement that all companies over a certain size have an audit (with small companies being exempt). The statutory external audit is therefore one of the most common forms of assurance engagements.

Definition

The objective of an audit of financial statements is to enable the auditor to express an opinion whether the financial statements are prepared, in all material respects, in accordance with an applicable financial reporting framework.

Worked example: Audit

The key criteria of an assurance engagement can be seen in an audit as follows:

- Three party involvement

    - The shareholders (users)
    - The board of directors (the responsible party)
    - The audit firm (the practitioner)

- Subject matter

    - The financial statements

- Relevant criteria

    - Law and accounting standards

- Evidence

    - As has been said earlier, sufficient and appropriate evidence is required to support an assurance opinion. The specific requirements in relation to evidence on assurance engagements will be looked at in Chapters 4 and 11.

- Written report in a suitable form

    - Again, as has been said, an assurance report is a written report issued in a prescribed form. We will look at the specific requirements for an audit report in Chapter 4.

The key outcome of the statutory audit is the audit opinion. In the UK, the auditor will normally express his audit opinion by reference to the 'true and fair view', which is an expression of reasonable assurance. Whilst this term is at the heart of the audit, 'true' and 'fair' are not defined in law or audit guidance. However, for practical purposes the following definitions are generally accepted.

Definitions

True: Information is factual and conforms with reality, not false. In addition the information conforms with required standards and law. The accounts have been correctly extracted from the books and records.

Fair: Information is free from discrimination and bias in compliance with expected standards and rules. The accounts should reflect the commercial substance of the company's underlying transactions.

4.2 Legal and professional requirements

Auditors in the UK are subject to both legal and professional requirements. The legal requirements are all contained within the Companies Act 2006.

The Companies Act requires that auditors are members of a Recognised Supervisory Body (RSB) and are eligible for appointment under the rules of that body. RSBs are required to have rules to ensure that those eligible for appointment as a company auditor are either:

- Individuals holding an appropriate qualification, or
- Firms controlled by qualified persons

The ICAEW is an RSB. Professional qualifications are a prerequisite of membership of an RSB, and these are offered by Registered Qualifying Bodies approved by the Secretary of State.

RSBs must also implement procedures for monitoring their registered auditors on a regular basis.

The Companies Act 2006 also sets out factors which make a person ineligible for being a company auditor, for example, if he or she is:

- An officer or employee of the company
- A partner or employee of such a person
- Any partner in a partnership in which such a person is a partner
- Ineligible by the above for appointment as auditor of any directly connected companies

As you will see later in this course, the professional ethics of the RSBs are usually far stricter in their criteria for ineligibility as an auditor.

In the UK, the Government has delegated the task of independent monitoring of the UK accountancy profession to the Financial Reporting Council (FRC). The FRC is responsible for issuing auditing standards, which it does through its Codes and Standards Committee. The FRC issues the following standards and guidance for auditing:

- Auditing standards
- Ethical standards for Auditors
- Practice notes
- Bulletins
- Standards for reviews of interim financial statements performed by the auditor of the entity

The auditing standards issued by the FRC are the International Standards on Auditing (ISAs), augmented for UK requirements. Note that until July 2012, the FRC's work in this area was done by the Auditing Practices Board (APB). Already existing guidance (eg ISAs) was issued by the APB and may still be referred to as such, and indeed the FRC has continued to refer to the APB in guidance issued since it ceased to exist.

ISA 200 (UK and Ireland) *Overall Objectives of the Independent Auditor and the Conduct of an Auditor in Accordance with International Standards on Auditing* states that auditors shall comply with relevant ethical requirements relating to audit engagements. These will be outlined later in this Study Manual. An auditor must conduct an audit in accordance with ISAs. Relevant ISAs will be referred to in this Study Manual.

4.3 International Standards on Auditing (ISAs)

As stated above, statutory audits conducted in the UK must be conducted in accordance with ISAs (UK and Ireland) as issued by the FRC. ISAs are made up of:

- Introductory material and definitions
- Objectives
- Requirements
- Application and other explanatory material (including appendices)

The requirements must be adhered to if an audit is to be conducted 'in accordance with ISAs' (as UK audits must be). That is to say, the basic principles and essential audit procedures required must be **applied** in the circumstances of each audit: this is where the 'application and other explanatory material' comes in. This part of an ISA is more concrete and practical, and sometimes contains examples of what the auditor must think about (and do) in practice.

The application material is an integral part of an ISA. It does not carry the same weight as the requirements because it may not be relevant in every case, but an auditor must make sure that an audit is conducted in the manner set out by the application guidance.

4.4 The value of the statutory audit

The reason why most companies that have audits do so, is that they are legally required to. However, audits can be invaluable to an entity because they may enhance the credibility of the financial statements, among other key benefits discussed in section 2 above.

4.5 Stages of an audit

In common with other assurance engagements, an audit will comprise several stages along the way to its eventual completion and the issuance of the auditor's opinion.

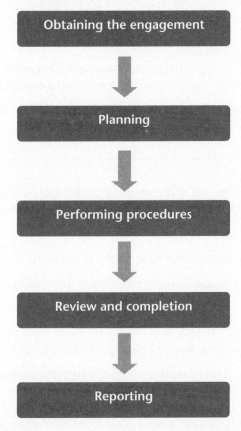

Before the engagement even begins, it must be obtained; there are various requirements that must be adhered to in relation to this which are covered in Chapter 2. It is important at this stage to consider the professional and ethical requirements around accepting audit engagements, and these are covered in Chapters 14, 15 and 16.

Planning is a crucial aspect of the audit, with the importance of proper planning being emphasised greatly by auditing standards (ISAs). This is covered in Chapter 3.

Audit procedures are designed at the planning stage, and are then performed in order to obtain evidence. Coverage of audit procedures pervades this Study Manual, but is concentrated in Chapters 6, 7 and 8.

Audit reporting is covered in Chapter 4, while review and completion are largely outside the scope of the Assurance syllabus and will be covered later on in your studies.

4.6 Overall objectives of the auditor

ISA 200 states that the overall objectives of the auditor are:

(a) To obtain reasonable assurance about whether the financial statements as a whole are free from material misstatement, whether due to fraud or error, thereby enabling the auditor to express an opinion on whether the financial statements are prepared, in all material respects, in accordance with an applicable financial reporting framework; and

(b) To report on the financial statements, and communicate as required by the ISAs, in accordance with the auditor's findings.

In order to do this, the auditor must:

- Comply with relevant ethical requirements

- Plan and perform the audit with professional scepticism

- Exercise professional judgement

- Obtain audit evidence that is both sufficient and appropriate, from which reasonable conclusions may be drawn, on which the auditor's opinion is then based

 ## Definitions

Professional scepticism is an attitude that includes a questioning mind, being alert to conditions which may indicate possible misstatement due to error or fraud, and a critical assessment of audit evidence.

Professional judgement is the application of relevant training, knowledge and experience in making informed decisions about the courses of action that are appropriate in the circumstances of the audit engagement.

ISA 200 states that auditors must plan and perform an audit with an attitude of professional scepticism, recognising that circumstances may exist that cause the financial statements to be materially misstated.

This requires the auditor to be alert to:

- Audit evidence that contradicts other audit evidence obtained

- Information that brings into question the reliability of documents and responses to inquiries to be used as audit evidence

- Conditions that may indicate possible fraud

- Circumstances that suggest the need for audit procedures in addition to those required by ISAs

Professional scepticism needs to be maintained throughout the audit to reduce the risks of overlooking unusual transactions, over-generalising when drawing conclusions, and using inappropriate assumptions in determining the nature, timing and extent of audit procedures and evaluating the results of them. Professional scepticism is also necessary to the critical assessment of audit evidence. This includes questioning contradictory audit evidence and the reliability of documents and responses from management and those charged with governance.

ISA 200 also requires the auditor to exercise professional judgement in planning and performing an audit of financial statements. Professional judgement is required in the following areas:

- Materiality and audit risk
- Nature, timing and extent of audit procedures
- Evaluation of whether sufficient appropriate audit evidence has been obtained
- Evaluating management's judgements in applying the applicable financial reporting framework
- Drawing conclusions based on the audit evidence obtained

Summary and Self-test

Summary

An assurance engagement is one in which a practitioner expresses a conclusion designed to enhance the degree of confidence of the intended users other than the responsible party about the outcome of the evaluation or measurement of a subject matter against criteria

Levels of assurance:
- Limited
- Reasonable (high)

Key elements:
- Three party relationship
- Subject matter
- Suitable criteria
- Sufficient appropriate evidence
- Written report

Key example: audit
Directors, auditors, shareholders
Financial statements
Law and accounting standards
As prescribed by ISA 500
Audit report

Benefits:
- Independent, professional opinion
- Added confidence to other users
- Deterrent to error/fraud

Limitations:
Subjective, sampled, limitations of systems, information from third parties, limitations of reporting, includes estimates

Self-test

Answer the following questions.

1   Assurance services are required by law.

☐   True

☐   False

2   What **five** elements are required for an engagement to be an assurance engagement?

1.....................................

2.....................................

3.....................................

4.....................................

5.....................................

3   Name **four** limitations of an assurance service.

1.....................................

2.....................................

3.....................................

4.....................................

4   Reasonable assurance is a high level of assurance.

☐   True

☐   False

Now, go back to the Learning Objectives in the Introduction. If you are satisfied you have achieved these objectives, please tick them off.

Answer to Interactive question 1

1 Three party involvement:

- Jamal (the intended user)
- You (the practitioner)
- The directors of Company X as they produce the financial statements (the responsible party)

2 Subject matter

The most recent financial statements of Company X are the subject matter

3 Relevant criteria

It is most likely in this instance that the criteria would be accounting standards, so that Jamal was assured that the financial statements were properly prepared and comparable with other companies' financial statements

4 Evidence

You would have to agree the extent of procedures in relation to this assignment with Jamal so that he knew the level of evidence you were intending to seek. This would depend on several factors, including the degree of secrecy in the proposed transaction and whether the directors of Company X allowed you to inspect the books and documents

5 Report

Again, the nature of the report would be agreed between you and Jamal, however, it would be a written report containing your opinion on the financial statements

Answer to Interactive question 2

An independent, professional opinion
Additional confidence given to other related parties
Assurance may act as a deterrent to error or fraud

1 False (an audit may be required by law if the company does not qualify as a small company)

2 1 Three party relationship
  2 Subject matter
  3 Suitable criteria
  4 Sufficient appropriate evidence
  5 Written report

3 From:

  1 Subjective exercise
  2 Sampling
  3 Limitations in systems
  4 Limitations in report
  5 Information from third parties
  6 Estimations

4 True

CHAPTER 2

Process of assurance: obtaining an engagement

Learning objectives

Tick off

- Be aware of how assurance firms obtain work

- Understand the key issues practitioners must consider before accepting engagements

- Know what a letter of engagement is and what it does

The specific syllabus reference for this chapter is: 1f.

Syllabus links

The issues of obtaining engagements will be looked at in much greater detail in the Audit and Assurance paper at the Application level.

Examination context

This is a fairly minor area for the exam, but you could expect at least one question on the scope of the engagement (there was a question about engagement letters in the sample paper) and possibly another on the considerations of the assurance firm when deciding to accept engagements.

In the assessment, candidates may be required to:

- Identify acceptance procedures
- Identify sources of information about new clients
- Select procedures required by money laundering legislation
- Determine the purpose of a letter of engagement

1 Obtaining an engagement

Section overview

- Accountants are permitted to advertise for clients, within certain professional guidelines.
- Accountants may sometimes be invited to tender for an audit.

How assurance firms obtain clients is an important practical question, but it is largely outside the scope of this syllabus. In brief, you should be aware that:

- Accountants are permitted to advertise for clients within certain professional guidelines, the details of which you do not need to know.

- Accountants are often invited to tender for particular engagements, which means that they offer a quote for services, outlining the benefits of their firm and personnel, usually in competition with other firms which are tendering at the same time.

In this syllabus, if the topics in this chapter are examined, it will be in the context of an accountant being invited by a potential client to accept an engagement. We will go on now to look at the things which an accountant must consider when he is so invited.

2 Accepting an engagement

Section overview

- The **present** and **proposed auditors** should normally **communicate** about the client prior to the audit being accepted.

- The client must be asked to give permission for communication to occur. If the client **refuses** to give **permission**, the proposed auditors should normally decline the appointment.

- The auditors must ensure they have sufficient resources (time and staff, for example) to carry out the appointment.

- The audit firm must have client due diligence procedures in place in order to comply with the Money Laundering Regulations 2007.

This section covers the procedures that the **auditors must** undertake to **ensure that their appointment is valid** and that they are clear to act.

2.1 Appointment considerations

Section 210 of the ICAEW Code of Ethics sets out the rules under which accountants should accept new appointments. Before a new audit client is accepted, the auditors must determine whether there are any **independence** or **other ethical issues** likely to cause significant problems with the ethical code (ie significant threats to complying with the fundamental principles of ethical behaviour – see later in this text). Furthermore, new auditors should ensure that they have been appointed in a proper and legal manner.

The nominee auditors must carry out the following procedures.

Acceptance procedures	
Ensure **professionally qualified** to act	Consider whether disqualified on legal or ethical grounds, for example if there would be a conflict of interest with another client. We will look in more detail at ethical issues later in this Study Manual.
Ensure **existing resources adequate**	Consider available time, staff and technical expertise.
Obtain references	Make independent enquiries if directors not personally known.
Communicate with present auditors	Enquire whether there are reasons/circumstances behind the change which the new auditors ought to know, also as a matter of courtesy.

Some of the basic factors for consideration are given below.

- The integrity of those managing a company will be of great importance, particularly if the company is controlled by one or a few dominant personalities.

- The audit firm will also consider whether the client is likely to be high or low risk to the firm in terms of being able to draw an appropriate assurance conclusion in relation to that client. The following table contrasts low and high risk clients.

Low risk	High risk
Good long-term prospects	Poor recent or forecast performance
Well-financed	Likely lack of finance
Strong internal controls	Significant control weaknesses
Conservative, prudent accounting policies	Evidence of questionable integrity, doubtful accounting policies
Competent, honest management	Lack of finance director
Few unusual transactions	Significant unexplained transactions or transactions with connected companies

Where the risk level of a company's audit is determined as anything other than low, then the specific risks should be identified and documented. It might be necessary to assign specialists in response to these risks, particularly industry specialists, as independent reviewers. Some audit firms have procedures for closely monitoring audits which have been accepted, but which are considered high risk.

Generally, the expected fees from a new client should reflect the **level of risk** expected. They should also offer the same sort of return expected of clients of this nature and reflect the overall financial strategy of the audit firm. Occasionally, the audit firm will want the work to gain entry into the client's particular industry, or to establish better contacts within that industry. These factors will all contribute to a total expected economic return.

The audit firm will generally want the relationship with a client to be **long term**. This is not only to enjoy receiving fees year after year; it is also to allow the audit work to be enhanced by better knowledge of the client and thereby offer a better service.

Conflict of interest problems can be significant; the firm should establish that no existing clients will cause difficulties as competitors of the new client. Other services to other clients may have an impact here, not just audit.

The audit firm must have the **resources** to perform the work properly, as well as any **specialist knowledge or skills**. The impact on existing engagements must be estimated, in terms of staff time and the timing of the audit.

Sources of information about new clients	
Enquiries of other sources	Bankers, solicitors
Review of **documents**	Most recent annual accounts, listing particulars, credit rating
Previous accountants/auditors	Previous auditors should be invited to disclose fully all relevant information
Review of **rules and standards**	Consider specific laws/standards that relate to industry

Prospective auditors should seek the prospective client's permission to contact the previous auditors. If this permission is not given, the prospective auditors should normally decline the appointment. Normally permission will be given, so the prospective auditors can write to the outgoing auditors.

Worked example: Initial communication

This is an example of an initial communication.

> To: Retiring & Co
>
> Chartered Accountants
>
> Dear Sir or Madam
>
> Re: New Client Co Ltd
>
> We have been asked to allow our name to go forward for nomination as auditors of the above company, and we should therefore be grateful if you would please let us know whether there are any professional reasons why we should not accept nomination ....
>
> Acquiring & Co
>
> Chartered Accountants, Registered Auditors

Having negotiated these steps the auditors will be in a position to accept the nomination, or not, as the case may be.

ICAEW

Worked example: Appointment decision chart

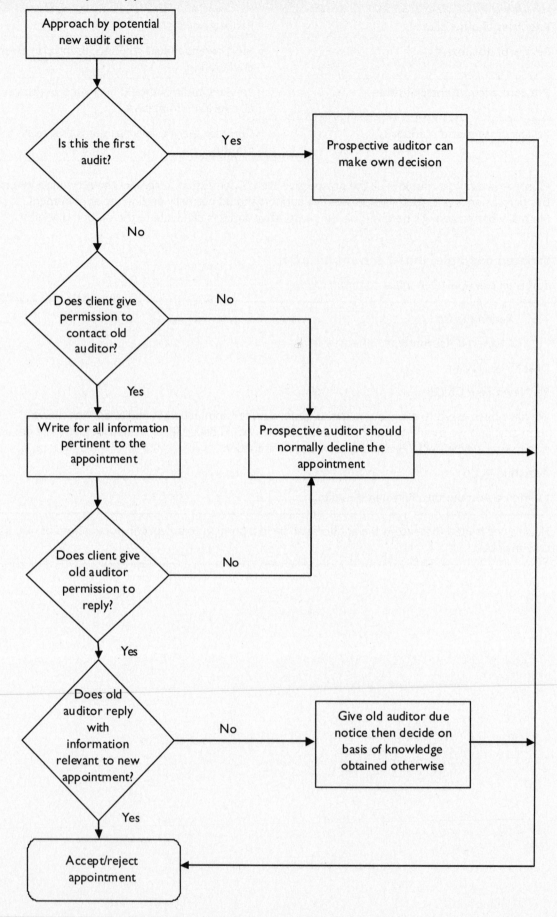

Approach by potential
new audit client

Is this the first
audit?

Yes → Prospective auditor can
make own decision

No

Does client give
permission to
contact old
auditor?

No → Prospective auditor should
normally decline the
appointment

Yes

Write for all information
pertinent to the
appointment

Does client give
old auditor
permission to
reply?

No

Does old
auditor reply
with
information
relevant to new
appointment?

No → Give old auditor due
notice then decide on
basis of knowledge
obtained otherwise

Yes

Accept/reject
appointment

Interactive question 1: Accepting appointment [Difficulty level: Easy]

Identify whether the following are true or false. The audit firm should consider the following factors when determining whether to accept an engagement.

	True	False
Whether the firm is ethically barred from acting.		
Whether the firm has sufficient resources to carry out the engagement.		
Whether the firm can make sufficient profit from the engagement.		
Whether the client is new to the firm.		
Whether the client gives permission to contact the outgoing auditors.		

See **Answer** at the end of this chapter.

The following procedures should be carried out after accepting nomination.

- **Ensure** that the **outgoing auditors' removal** or **resignation** has been **properly conducted** in accordance with national legislation.

 The new auditors should see a valid notice of the outgoing auditors' resignation, or confirm that the outgoing auditors were properly removed.

- **Ensure** that the **new auditors' appointment is valid**. The new auditors should obtain a copy of the resolution passed at the general meeting appointing them as the company's auditors.

- Set up and **submit a letter of engagement** to the directors of the company.

Where the outgoing auditors have fees still owing by the client, the new auditors need not decline appointment solely for this reason.

Once a new appointment has taken place, the **new auditors should obtain all books and papers which belong to the client from the outgoing auditors**. The outgoing auditors should ensure that all such documents are transferred promptly, **unless** they have a lien (a legal right to hold on to them) because of unpaid fees. An outgoing auditor cannot have a lien over the accounting records of a registered company as the Companies Act requires these to be available for public inspection. The outgoing auditors should also pass any useful information to the new auditors if it will be of help, without charge, unless a lot of work is involved.

2.2 Other assurance engagements

Similar considerations will be required for any assurance engagements. The legal considerations relating to audit will not be relevant to other assurance engagements, but the ethical, risk and practical considerations will be just as valid.

2.3 Money laundering regulations

In order to comply with the Money Laundering Regulations 2007, assurance firms must keep certain records about clients and undertake what is known as client due diligence.

It is mandatory to check the identity of all clients before any work is undertaken when an ongoing relationship is envisaged (this would be the case for certain assurance engagements) or where a one-off transaction or a series of transactions greater than €15,000 will take place.

The identity of clients should be checked by:

- **For individuals**: obtaining official documents including a photograph and identifying the client's full name and permanent address, for example, a passport supported by a number of utilities bills or a driving licence.

- **For companies**: obtaining similar legal information from the Registrar of Companies, for example, a certificate of incorporation, the registered address and a list of shareholders and directors.

Client identification documents must be kept for a minimum of five years and until five years have elapsed since the relationship with the client in question has ceased. It is also necessary to keep a full audit trail of all transactions with the client.

Interactive question 2: Client due diligence   [Difficulty level: Easy]

Drew Brothers, chartered accountants, has recently accepted appointment as the auditor of Abysin Ltd. In terms of client due diligence, they should check which **two** of the following documents?

☐ Certificate of incorporation

☐ Passport

☐ Utilities bills

☐ Annual return

See **Answer** at the end of this chapter.

3 Agreeing terms of an engagement

Section overview

- An engagement letter should be sent to all clients to clarify the terms of the engagement.

- Agreement of audit engagement terms must be in writing.

- It must include an explanation of the scope of the audit, the limitations of an audit and the responsibilities of auditors and those charged with governance.

- It may contain other information concerning practical details of the audit.

The purpose of an engagement letter is to:

- Define clearly the **extent** of the firm's **responsibilities** and so minimise the possibility of any misunderstanding between the client and the firm

- Provide **written confirmation** of the firm's **acceptance** of the appointment, the scope of the engagement and the form of their report

If an engagement letter is not sent to clients, both new and existing, there is scope for argument about the precise extent of the respective obligations of the client and its directors and the auditors. The elements of an engagement letter should be discussed and agreed with management before it is sent.

An engagement letter for any type of assurance engagement will contain the same contents as an audit engagement letter (discussed below). Clearly details will be different (for instance, it will cover the **scope** of the engagement, but the scope of an audit and the scope of a review of forecast information, for example, will be different). An engagement letter for an assurance engagement other than audit is likely to refer to specific fees for the engagement. As you will see below, as an audit engagement is often recurring, specific fees are initially not mentioned.

3.1 Audit engagement letters

ISA 210 (UK and Ireland) *Agreeing the Terms of Audit Engagements* requires that the auditor and the client agree on the terms of the engagement. The agreed terms must be in writing and the usual form would be a **letter of engagement**. Any other form of appropriate contract, however, may be used.

Even in countries where the audit objectives and scope and the auditor's obligations are established by law, an **audit engagement letter** may be informative for clients.

The auditors should send an engagement letter to all new clients soon **after their appointment** as auditors and, in any event, before the commencement of the first audit assignment. They should also consider sending an engagement letter to existing clients to whom no letter has previously been sent as soon as a suitable opportunity presents itself.

The following items shall be included in the engagement letter.

- The **objective** of the **audit** of financial statements.

- The **scope** of the audit, which could include reference to applicable legislation, regulations, or pronouncements of professional bodies to which the auditor adheres.

- The **auditor's responsibility**.

- The **reporting framework** that is applicable for the financial statements being prepared, for example International Financial Reporting Standards.

- **Management's responsibility** to prepare the financial statements and to provide the auditor with **unrestricted access** to whatever records, documentation and other information is requested in connection with the audit.

- The form of any **reports** of results of the engagement.

The form and remaining content of audit engagement letters may vary for each client, but the auditor may wish to include in the letter the following items.

- The form of any **other communication** of the results of the engagement.

- The fact that because of the **test nature** and other **inherent limitations** of an audit, together with the inherent limitations of any accounting and internal control system, there is an unavoidable risk that some material misstatements may remain undiscovered.

- Arrangements regarding the **planning** of the audit.

- Expectation of receiving from management **written confirmation** of **representations** made in connection with the audit.

- Agreement of the client to provide the auditor with information in time to allow the auditor to complete the audit in line with the proposed timetable.

- Basis on which **fees** are computed and any billing arrangements.

- Request for the client to **confirm the terms** of the engagement by acknowledging receipt of the engagement letter.

When relevant, the following points could also be made.

- Arrangements concerning the involvement of **other auditors** and **experts** in some aspects of the audit.

- Arrangements concerning the involvement of **internal auditors** and other client staff.

- Arrangements to be made with the **predecessor auditor**, if any, in the case of an initial audit.

- Any **restriction of the auditor's liability** when such possibility exists.

- A reference to any **further agreements** between the auditor and the client.

- Any obligations to provide audit working papers to **other parties**.

Worked example: Audit engagement letter (extract)

To the Board of Directors of ABC Company

ACTING AS AUDITORS UNDER THE COMPANIES ACT 2006

RESPONSIBILITIES AND SCOPE FOR AUDIT SERVICES

Your responsibilities as directors

As directors of the company, you are responsible for preparing financial statements which give a true and fair view and which have been prepared in accordance with the Companies Act 2006 (the Act). As directors you must not approve the financial statements unless you are satisfied that they give a true and fair view of the assets, liabilities, financial position and profit or loss of the company.

In preparing the financial statements, you are required to:

- Select suitable accounting policies and then apply them consistently;

- Make judgements and estimates that are reasonable and prudent; and

- Prepare the financial statements on the going concern basis unless it is inappropriate to presume that the company will continue in business.

You are responsible for keeping adequate accounting records that set out with reasonable accuracy at any time the company's financial position, and for ensuring that the financial statements comply with International Financial Reporting Standards (IFRSs) as adopted by the European Union and with the Companies Act 2006 and give a true and fair view.

You are also responsible for such internal control as you determine is necessary to enable the preparation of financial statements that are free from material misstatement whether due to fraud or error.

You are also responsible for safeguarding the assets of the company and hence for taking reasonable steps to prevent and detect fraud and other irregularities.

You are responsible for ensuring that the company complies with laws and regulations that apply to its activities, and for preventing non-compliance and detecting any that occurs.

You have undertaken to make available to us, as and when required, all the company's accounting records and related financial information, including minutes of management and shareholders' meetings, that we need to do our work. You have also undertaken to provide us with unrestricted access to any persons from whom we deem it necessary to obtain audit evidence. Each director is required to take all steps that he ought to take as a director in order to make himself aware of any relevant audit information and to establish that we are aware of that information.

Our responsibilities as auditor

We have a statutory responsibility to report to the members as a body, whether in our opinion the financial statements have been properly prepared in accordance with IFRSs, whether they have been prepared in accordance with the Companies Act 2006 and whether they give a true and fair view. We are also required to report whether the information given in the directors' report is consistent with the financial statements. In arriving at our opinion, we are required to consider the following matters, and report on any that we are not satisfied with:

(a) Whether the company has kept adequate accounting records, and whether branches that we have not visited have sent in returns adequate for our audit;

(b) Whether the company's individual accounts are in agreement with the accounting records and returns; and

(c) Whether we have obtained all the information and explanations which we consider necessary for the purposes of our audit.

We may also need to deal with certain other matters in our report. If the company prepares accounts and reports in accordance with the small companies regime when in our opinion it is not entitled to do so we are required to state that fact in our report.

We have a professional responsibility to report if the financial statements do not significantly comply with applicable financial reporting standards, unless we believe there is a good reason for the non-compliance. In deciding whether or not this is the case, we consider:

(a) Whether the non-compliance is necessary for the financial statements to give a true and fair view; and

(b) Whether the non-compliance has been clearly disclosed.

We also have a professional responsibility to consider whether other information in documents containing audited financial statements is consistent with those financial statements.

Scope of audit

We will carry out our audit in accordance with the International Standards of Auditing (UK and Ireland) issued by the Financial Reporting Council. Those Standards require that we comply with ethical requirements and plan and perform the audit to obtain reasonable assurance about whether the financial statements are free of material misstatements. An audit involves performing procedures to obtain audit evidence about the amounts and disclosures in the financial statements. The procedures selected depend on the auditors' judgment, including the assessment of the risks of material misstatement of the financial statements, whether due to fraud or error. An audit also includes evaluating the appropriateness of accounting policies used and the reasonableness of accounting estimates made by management, as well as evaluating the overall presentation of the financial statements. Because of the test nature and other inherent limitations of an audit, together with the inherent limitations of any accounting and internal control system, there is an unavoidable risk that even some material misstatements may remain undiscovered.

We shall obtain an understanding of the accounting and internal control systems in order to assess their adequacy as a basis for the preparation of the financial statements and to establish whether adequate accounting records have been maintained by the company. We shall expect to obtain such appropriate evidence as we consider sufficient to enable us to draw reasonable conclusions there from. In addition to our report on the financial statements, we will provide you with a separate letter concerning any significant deficiencies in accounting and internal control systems which come to our notice.

The nature and extent of our audit will vary according to our assessment of the company's accounting system and, where we wish to rely on it the internal control system, and may cover any aspect of the business's operations that we consider appropriate. Our audit is not designed to identify all significant deficiencies in the company's systems and internal controls but, if we detect significant deficiencies we will report them to you in writing.

As part of our normal audit procedures, we may ask you to confirm in writing representations you have made to us during the audit. In particular, where misstatements in the financial statements that we bring to your attention are not adjusted, you must state your reasons. In connection with representations and the supply of information to us generally, we draw your attention to section 501 of the Companies Act 2006 under which it is an offence for anyone to recklessly or knowingly supply information to the auditors that is false or misleading and to fail to promptly provide information requested.

To help us examine your financial statements, we will ask to see all documents or statements that are due to be issued with the financial statements. We are also entitled to receive details of all written resolutions that are to be circulated to members, to attend all the company's general meetings and to receive notice of them all.

You are responsible for safeguarding the company's assets and for preventing and detecting fraud, error and non-compliance with law or regulations. We will plan our audit so that we can reasonably expect to detect significant misstatements in the financial statements or accounting records (including those resulting from fraud, error or non-compliance with law or regulations), but you cannot rely on us finding all such errors.

In respect of the expected form and content of our report, we refer you to the most recent bulletin on auditors' reports published by the Auditing Practices Board at http://www.frc.org.uk/apb. The form and content of our report may need to be amended in the light of our findings.

Once we have issued our report, we have no further responsibility in relation to the financial statements for that financial year. However, we expect that you will inform us of any material event occurring between the date of our report and the date the financial statements are sent out in accordance with section 423 Companies Act 2006 which may affect the financial statements.

We look forward to full cooperation from your staff during our audit.

[Other relevant information]

[Insert other information, such as fee arrangements, billings and other specific terms, as appropriate.]

XYZ & Co.

Acknowledged and agreed on behalf of ABC Company by
(signed)
....
Name and Title

Interactive question 3: Engagement letters [Difficulty level: Exam standard]

Which **three** of the following may be contained within a letter of engagement?

- [ ] Responsibilities of the auditors
- [ ] Responsibilities of the directors
- [ ] The names of the staff assigned to the engagement
- [ ] The scope of the audit

See **Answer** at the end of this chapter.